"I read your book and it is excellent. Thank you for sharing your experience. It helps!"
  —Stephanie Cunningham, MSW
  California

"I have never found a book quite like this. Besides taking the reader on the author's own personal journey, it provides insights into the grieving process as well as many practical suggestions for dealing with loss in a supportive and gentle way. There are opportunities for journaling and reflecting to help the reader work through the pain and heartache of loss. A remarkable, helpful book."
  —Robin Brown, retired school teacher
  California

"I have found it both personally and professionally to be a great source of comfort. The comfort comes from reading that it's ok.... it's ok to feel whatever it is that I'm feeling or not feeling! It's very helpful, a guiding light; a beacon through the storm!"
  —Frances Knight, intuitive counselor
  New Zealand

"As a reader who has contemplated suicide, the author's intimate view of the pain and anguish left behind has opened my mind and heart to the full circle of such action. My thanks and gratitude to Ms WolfKlain."
  —Judith Casteel, fiber artist
  California

GOING FORWARD

Living Life After Loss

GOING FORWARD

Living Life After Loss

Lisa WolfKlain

TREE LEAF PUBLISHING

Print ISBN 978-0-9981960-6-0
eBook ISBN 978-0-9981960-7-7

First Printing 2017
Printed and bound in United States of America

Cover Illustration: Cheney LaRue
Author photo: Tracy Martin Photography
Cover design/Interior design: Jim Shubin, bookalchemist.net

I dedicate this to my husband Matthew and our
children: Melissa, Tyler, Ben, and Ashley.
They give me the foundation of love, respect, and trust
from which I can write these words.

Thank you Deborah Kroll. You helped me integrate my
new reality with spirit.

Thank you Cheney LaRue for your brilliant artwork.

Thank you to my wonderful group of readers who
provided me with guidance and support throughout the
writing process.

Introduction

A mother who loses a child is never the same again. My son Ben, at age twenty seven, took his own life.

The first few weeks after his death were a blur of taking care of the business of death: picking up his things at the coroner, planning and having the memorial service, receiving all the friends and family that came or stopped by. When these were over, I searched and searched for books or information that would help me get through the day. I couldn't find any that worked for me. So I wrote this book. These words come from my experience. They are not based on research though, as Carl Rogers said, "What is most personal is general." My hope is that it will help you through your loss, whatever it may be.

This book features two parallel parts: my thoughts and a journal. At the end of each chapter you will find questions and space to write, draw, paste photos or whatever you are moved to do. The journal part can be used or skipped over. Feel free to add more pages if you need more space or you may prefer to begin a blank journal of your own, rather than writing in this book. I hope you will find the questions helpful springboards to get you started as you go forward on your journey.

Most of all I wish you—peace, solace, self-care and self-discovery.

—Lisa WolfKlain

Ben was about 11. He and I had a four-hour drive coming home from a soccer tournament. At one point there was a bridge in the distance.

He asked me,
 "How far can you see?"

 And then he said:

"Up to the sky, a great distance

 On the horizon not so far; peaks, valleys change the view.

 Above the horizon, I see mountains.

 Into the fog, out of the fog

 Dark fog, light fog

 Driving in the fog, no sense of the bridge

 Seems forever until—surprise, it is here."

Note I found in Ben's handwriting after his death:
 "When I am right I am right

 When I'm wrong I could have been right

 So I'm right 'cause I could have been wrong."

From *The Prophet* by Kahlil Gibran:

Your children are not your children.

They are the sons and daughters of life's longing for itself.

They come through you, not from you.

And though they are with you, they belong not to you.

You may give them your love, but not your thoughts.

For they have their own thoughts.

You may house their bodies but not their souls.

Table of Contents

Part I
The Loss

Chapter 1

Loss

The rage, the pain, the heartbreak, the anger.

I wake up in Hiroshima, Japan. The phone is blinking.

The day before, my husband and I had visited the museum depicting the death, destruction, and horrors of the atomic bomb. We found it deeply moving learning about the terrible losses the people of this city had endured. We were emotionally exhausted. That evening we had gone to an American-style restaurant owned by a man from Nepal. We chatted with the owner, laughed, and talked about our family. After thirty-two years together, I had learned something new—my husband gets the hiccups when he eats something really, really spicy. We had a wonderful time.

I had spent the week working in Tokyo, training plant managers from an international firm in strategic communication. It had been fun working with these men, who spoke seven different languages. My husband had joined me two days earlier to spend another week traveling in Japan. Traveling together is one of the things we love to do.

We got back to our hotel and fell into bed. My husband's phone kept going off in the night, and at one point I asked him to turn the ringer off. With the time change, I figured the people he played games with were telling him it was his turn.

The next morning we find urgent text messages: "Call home", "family emergency." The thought runs through my head that something must have happened to my husband's parents, who are in their nineties. We only have data and no phone coverage, so I ask my brother who has sent the texts to email the message.

The email comes back: "Ben died. He hanged himself in his garage" (in the house he shared with a friend and his brother, who found him).

No, no, no! Our twenty seven year-old beautiful baby boy. We collapse in overwhelming grief. My husband, who is gentle and kind, hurls his phone across the bed. I pick up the hotel phone to call my brother...

In a split second my life as I know it is over—never, never to be the same.

Traveling home is a blur. We cannot fly home that day

and have to rearrange our entire schedule. It takes us two days to catch a flight from Narita Airport to San Francisco. On the train from Hiroshima to Tokyo we sit in silence, holding hands, stunned. Nothing but sadness. I cannot think, though there is so much that needs to be done to get us home: change our airline tickets, spend the night in Tokyo, pick up a bag I left there from my work, waste time until our 5 pm flight the following day. What about our other adult children back home? We talk on the phone, crying while setting up arrangements for his body. Decisions.

My sister-in-law and her husband come to stay at our house with our children. It is her birthday. He died on her birthday. How can she forgive us?

Our oldest daughter steps in to make arrangements. She is an actor and leaves her out-of-town show to make calls and send emails. She cancels our hotel reservations and makes an appointment with the funeral home. She takes control of things we cannot do as we speed our way to our California town.

All I want to do is hold my children. I start thinking of the pain they are in. We all knew that Ben was changing. We all tried to talk to him. He didn't want help. We did not want to push him away. I knew that the next few days would be extremely difficult for all of us. Ideas for guidelines start popping into my head for our family--now five-- to follow as we move through the next few weeks and beyond:

- No blame, no shame. We did what we could to love and help Ben.

- It is okay to say "I can't." "Can't make a decision." "Can't say anything at the memorial." "Can't talk right now." And we will not ask why. There will be no judging.

- We will grieve individually and together. We will grieve differently. We will pay attention to our expectations of each other in our grief.

- It is okay to behave any way we need to.

Finally home. Our family wraps our arms around each other in one big hug and cries. I tell them my "rules" for each other...they nod. I am relieved to be home, engulfing each other in our arms, knowing together we will do what we have to do.

And wonder, after that, how do we go on?

Pain is inevitable, suffering optional
∽ Source Unknown

Chapter 2

Grief

Divorce, death, job change, a move, injury.

Life brings us many challenges. Some are easy. We pick ourselves up, dust ourselves off, and away we go. Others present opportunities to change direction toward something better. Still others permanently shift our reality. These kinds of experiences create such monumental changes in us and in our world that we simply can't ever reflect on a time in the past or see a place and re-experience it as it was. After great loss a task we used to do takes on a new context and can't be experienced in the same way. The loss changes us forever.

Grief is like a fog. You know it is there—the pain, the absence. It clouds and touches everything. Sometimes the fog is very dark and so thick we cannot see our way through it. Other times the sun peeks through and illuminates our way as we create our path.

In the first year after Ben died I would crumble to the floor and scream and cry with sorrow. My entire world had been turned upside down. How could I go on without him in my life? The last two years that he was alive, I would see him every day as he worked on our house, remodeling and creating new spaces in his childhood home. I no longer had my son, my helper, my companion, listening to sports talk radio as he worked. No longer did I hear him come through the front door and say "Hey Ma." It was silent, empty, nothingness. Where was his smile? Lost. Gone. No longer. Never to see it again. Never to talk over a project or share his exploits in his softball game. Never dance with him on vacation or at a wedding. Never to see him grow old, maybe have children, live his life, expand his creativity. He was gone, silent. I could not find my way through the fog. It was closing in on me and weighing me down. I wailed like a ship horn trying to find my way through it, trying to figure out how I was going to live my life in his absence. It was all gray.

As time goes on the pain is not as harsh. I no longer wail, though I do cry, and I am sure I will always cry. Grief is a continual process. Grief will return. I have come to think of the loss as a hole in my heart. Sometimes it feels the size of a pinprick. At other times it feels like a chasm where grief floods back in. I was at a wedding sitting next to a gentleman who had lost his wife to cancer 15 years before. He told me that they had gone to Duke University together. A while before this he was watching Duke play basketball, and all of a sudden he started tearing up. He could not believe it. That pinprick of a hole had opened, and there was the grief again.

Something will happen—a memory, an action, a situation—when I will painfully connect to Ben being gone, and I will cry. His absence is always with me. I think about him every day, though it is no longer as painful. Over time the hole stays small. I can laugh and smile again.

What do we do to guide us through the fog of our grief? We need to allow ourselves to feel our emotions whenever and wherever they come, give ourselves permission to cry, talk about it, and be honest with ourselves about how we feel.

Similarly, we need to allow ourselves to feel happiness.

It is okay to be happy. We are not being disrespectful or forgetting the person we love by enjoying life, or laughing at funny or happy memories of that person. We need to live a life that still includes joy. I may never feel the extreme joy I used to feel, and I now know a new level of deep sadness. But I know Ben sees me and wants me to be happy, so I will allow myself to feel.

WRITE YOUR STORY OF LOSS

Of all the music that reaches furthest into heaven, it is the beating of a loving heart.

∾ Henry Ward Beecher

Chapter 3

Remembering

It's okay to cry when we are sad and okay to remember. Memories can be very comforting. At first it was very hard to think of Ben. Only sadness came over me. Now I am able to also remember happy times.

It is okay to keep things that remind us of the person we lost. I have some old cigarette butts, a used paper towel that he blew his nose on, his Chapstick, some pens, his hats, his necklace, and some clothes. We still have his ashes in his childhood room, along with some photos and some of his belongings. It brings me comfort to go into that space and talk to him while I am looking at his things. Some would call this a shrine. As long as having these things does not keep me in the past, or cause me to dream about what the future might have been, I believe it is okay and healthy. In my extended family we can sit around and share stories of him, and, in time, it has become easier.

The first Christmas after Ben died his brother gave me and my two daughters each a necklace with his name on it. I wear it every day. For me it represents love, love that the brothers shared and the love that they have for us. That same Christmas we were surprised to find two wonderfully wrapped packages on our doorstep. One was an angel from Ben's first girlfriend and her brother. The second was from an artist friend of his—a large, beautiful chalk drawing that shows his gorgeous smile.

His friends have honored him in many ways. Immediately after his death, two of his friends—one who has since died—got full upper-arm tattoos that represented something important to Ben, and one of his best friends got a large tattoo of a howling wolf in the same place a couple of years later. Another of his friends was going to ask Ben to be a groomsman at his wedding, and he still left a place for him. One of the bridesmaids walked down the aisle without an escort. One friend composed a song for him. His childhood friends started a flag football team and called themselves "24", Ben's football number. For me these gestures show the love that so many felt for him and the meaning he had brought to their lives.

After Ben's death one friend asked where he would be buried so that they could visit. We had his body cremated and we did not know where we wanted to put his ashes, so we decided to dedicate a bench at his high school on the track and football field. He was an exceptional athlete. It is a spot where he was very happy competing, and it holds great memories for all of us. It also provides a space for the community to sit and relax and for friends and family to gather.

At his memorial many of the people who knew Ben remembered him as a very thoughtful person who would help a friend in need or just listen to them. Some credited him for helping them stay out of gangs or jail. Another friend mentioned he wanted to seek counseling. I encouraged him though later thought, how is he going to pay for it? So my husband and I started The Ben Fund, a nonprofit that helps pay for counseling with licensed therapists for adults in our community between twenty and thirty years of age. We wanted to continue Ben's legacy as a very supportive friend by providing a way for others to talk with a counselor about their lives, regardless of the topic or challenges they faced.

Around the third anniversary of his death I asked his friends to send me favorite memories about Ben's mannerisms, what he laughed about, and any other remembrances they could offer. I felt my memory of him was fading over time, and I wanted to capture as much as possible. This has helped me keep my memories alive. I sometimes re-read their messages and cry, though it helps me to be thankful for what we had. We were lucky to have shared our lives, however briefly.

My next act of remembrance will be to have his name tattooed inside my wrist when I have this book published. It has been important for us to keep his memory alive and continue to promote his generosity of spirit in the community. I also believe it has helped us go forward.

WHAT DO YOU WANT TO REMEMBER ABOUT THE PERSON YOU HAVE LOST?

How will you capture these remembrances?

The world breaks everyone and afterward some
are strong at the broken places.
∾ Ernest Hemingway

Chapter 4

Making Peace with Our Loss

What does it mean to make peace with our loss? Many times we keep reliving the past and are awash with regrets and guilt and anger.

Anger is a natural response when we feel abandoned, betrayed, dismissed and/or forgotten. With suicide we can be angry at the person and ask, "Why did he leave us? Weren't we good enough? Didn't he love us? How could he cause us so much pain? People will think we were bad parents and that we didn't get him help, stop him, or somehow prevent what happened."

I know that overcoming this anger is very difficult, and I am not sure all of us in our family have come to terms with it. For me, for some reason, anger was a flash of emotion that passed quickly and then turned into sorrow.

I know he loved me and our family. I know he enjoyed being with us. I know he did not think of the consequences of his action as he took his own life. He was not thinking of us. He was immersed in his own pain and, for reasons I will never know, he did what he did. I don't think, if I could ask him, he could articulate the reasons. I believe he was only feeling and not thinking. He acted in the moment. For this moment of pain I feel sorrow that he had experienced so desperate a feeling that taking his own life was the only answer he could find for himself. My thoughts turn to wondering what I could have done to make him love himself more.

What could we have done differently? With the loss of a job we may be asking ourselves, "Should I have been more aggressive in managing my career and looked for other opportunities sooner?" In retirement we may feel a loss of identity and ask, "Was it the right decision? Was I really ready?" Following the death of a spouse we may learn things that may break our trust or bring on shame. We may ask, "What warning signs did I miss? What questions should I have asked?" And after any death we may wonder if we told the person we loved them enough or reconciled any differences in time.

Just as we need to accept that we have experienced a loss, we need to accept all that previously happened. The past is past, and we need to forgive ourselves, knowing that we did what we could at the time. We can acknowledge any regrets we may have, but then must let them go. Continually thinking of them will not change anything. Life cannot be reversed, though we can learn from it.

Learning from the past is different than reliving it.

We cannot go back and change what happened; however, we may be able to learn from the past by considering the consequences of our words and actions. Everything we say or do has an impact or consequence, which can be positive or negative. If we have had a negative impact, we can reflect on it and figure out how to do things differently in the future. Sometimes we can repair any lingering negative consequences. At the very least we can apologize for any harm we have caused.

Could I have done more for Ben? I talked to him about changes I saw in his behavior. I gave him articles and information. I consciously tried not to push too hard, which may have driven him away. Could I have done more? Should I have had another conversation that I did not get the chance to have? I am not infallible and did not do everything perfectly, though I did what I could at the time, and that is all I could do.

Avoid turning regrets into guilt. Guilt is when you feel responsible for causing the actions of others.

Whatever the circumstances of our loss, there are some things in life we can control entirely. Some things we can influence. And there are some things over which we have no control. The loss itself is, more often than not, something over which we have no control. If we have no control, then the only thing we can do is to accept it. The one thing in life we have total control over is ourselves—

the actions we take and the decisions we make. My son took his own life. That was beyond my control. I, and all my family, had talked to him, expressed concern to him, and used our influence to try to help him see what was going on from our perspective. That is all we could do.

We may have to actively forgive ourselves for actions we did or did not take, such as reconciling differences or paying attention to warning signs, or for words we did or did not say. "What if..." scenarios would probably not have changed the outcome of our loss; we don't know. So how do we forgive ourselves?

We must feel the anguish of what we are thinking or feeling. Sit and cry. Wail for what we perceive we should have done or could have done, whatever is causing the regret. Say it out loud. Apologize out loud and in our thoughts. Then expel the emotion and go to the logical side of our being. The biggest thing to remember is that all of that is in the past, and this is now. The past is over and done. We may have to think of this every day, whenever the "what if" thoughts come into our head, to remember we did the best we could at the time.

We must forgive ourselves for what we might have done.

Ultimately, as a twenty-seven year-old man, Ben was on his own journey, and I could not change that. Coming to this conclusion was not easy. Knowing I can only shape my own life, and not his, helped me to understand and find some peace.

WHAT IS HARD TO ACCEPT ABOUT THE LOSS?

WHAT IS HOLDING YOU BACK FROM MAKING PEACE WITH YOURSELF?

How can you forgive yourself for your perceived wrongs?

WHAT ARE THE EMOTIONS YOU ARE CARRYING AROUND?

Part II
Going Forward

Your living is determined not so much by what life brings to you
as by the attitude you bring to life; not so much by what
happens to you as by the way your mind looks at what happens.

∞ Kahlil Gibran

Chapter 5

New Reality

"Move on, get past it." "It's been two, three, four years, you should be over it by now." "How long is it going to take for you to—?"

What does this mean? That the loss is in the past, so move on? Forget about it? Get back to "normal" life?

We have heard these phrases from people. We may even have said them ourselves. This is the message our popular culture gives us. We need to strike them from our collective vocabulary. If we are waiting to "get over it", that time will never come. Yes, it did happen, and yes, it is in the past. But the loss is with us going forward and will be with us forever.

I do not like the word "healing" as it relates to loss. Healing to me means making it all better, as though the wound closes up and we are "normal." The illness is cured and we are fine. We are not healed after loss. Nothing will be "normal", nothing will be cured. Nothing is healed. Yes, the pain may not be as acute, but it is always there. It is that shrinking and expanding hole in our heart.

Our world is now changed. The pain becomes part of us. We do not forget, and we do not stop feeling. We learn to live differently. We are living a new reality. A new definition of life is forming. We do not heal or recover. We live differently. We remain alive and strive to find new meaning.

For much of our life the things that happen to us add to our story. We may go to a new school, get married, secure a job, buy a house, have children. When these life events happen it changes us, sometimes dramatically, often for the better. We do not even think about it. We are growing, expanding, and experiencing new and exciting things.

Death changes us too, but with loss something has been taken away. With death what we lose will never be replaced. This new reality is not exciting. We have lost a part of us that will not be growing back, it will always be missing.

People ask me how I am doing. I say "okay". I say, "Really, I am fine". Will I ever say "I'm fantastic"? I don't know if I said that even when Ben was alive. My new reality may have the same range of emotion as before, but the lows are much lower and the highs not as high. I live on a slightly different emotional continuum. Will it ever change? I don't know.

I know we can shape each day by how we move through, and with, this pain. We are creating another version of ourselves, one that did not exist before. We will recognize parts of ourselves and our life as we knew it, though it will never be as it was.

My loss has made a permanent impact on the way I see and experience the world. I pay attention to more small things: a new flower stalk blooming on a plant that never bloomed before, an invitation from a friend that I did not expect, an email from someone far away, a surprise in the mail, a cacophony of crows carrying on, the sun creating a rainbow on the ceiling, good news from one of my children, my husband saying " I love you", inspiration on a new project, a card from my mother-in-law, a hawk flying overheard in slow circles.

We are not starting our life over. We are starting another part of our journey. We have taken a road we did not know existed and did not choose. On this road we have to use the emotional wisdom we have gained through our loss as we go forward. It is an opportunity for us to find new meaning in life.

WHAT HAS CHANGED IN HOW YOU VIEW YOUR LIFE?

WHAT DO YOU WANT TO HOLD ON TO FROM YOUR "OLD LIFE"?

_____

_____

_____

_____

_____

_____

_____

_____

_____

_____

_____

_____

_____

_____

_____

HOW DO YOU SEE YOURSELF LIVING IN YOUR NEW REALITY?

_____

_____

_____

_____

_____

_____

_____

_____

_____

_____

_____

_____

_____

_____

I thought I could change the world. It took me a hundred years
to figure out I can't change the world.
I can only change Bessie. And, honey, that ain't easy either.

∽ Annie Elizabeth "Bessie" Delany, age 104

Chapter 6

Choice

As we go forward we wake up in our new reality every day. And every minute, every second of that day, we make choices about how to live. We can choose to get dressed and engage in the world, to talk about our loss, to tell the truth about our new life, and/or to convey our real feelings. We can choose to keep busy, pretend nothing has changed, maybe block out how we feel. Or we can choose to do nothing but sit and sink into the grief.

Loss is something that happens to us. Change is what we create.

We can choose to enjoy life without feeling guilty. Sometimes I think, "Why am I happy in this moment? I shouldn't be; my son's not here." But Ben wouldn't want me to be sad all the time. He loves me and would want me to find joy.

We can make something out of life for ourselves. We do not need to do something monumental. We can read a book or get out of the house. We all suffer, but how we handle it is up to us. For instance, if we are bored we can start a project or take a walk. If we are overwhelmed, we can slow down, seek solitude. If we become isolated we can get involved with others. Taking action will help shift our energy and jump-start our going forward.

A loss forces us to reevaluate our life—how we live, what we do, and what we value. Socrates believed that the unexamined life, the life of those who know nothing of themselves or their real needs and desires, is not worthy of being lived. Many of us do not take the time to make this examination. Loss gives us the opportunity and, in a way, permission to do so.

Going forward after loss is a time we can discover our self, our core. Life as we knew it is changed, altered, different, gone. Some aspects are still there. The more devastating the loss, the more things change, and the more life can be new again. We can have a new way of going forward on this part of our journey. We can take a fresh look because our perspective is changed. We can experience an opening that may not have been there before. We may pay attention to the world around us in new ways.

To help me figure out what I wanted my life to be going forward I did an inventory of where I found joy, peace, and fulfillment, and what was important to me. I know we have to do some things, like earn money to pay our bills; but how we do them, and how we spend our time, is what I can choose.

I asked myself these questions and listened to my thoughts and feeling:

- What is different in my new reality besides the loss?
- How do I want to live?
- Where do I find rejuvenation?
- What do I cherish, value?
- Whom do I love?
- What do I enjoy doing?
- What makes me happy?
- Where do I go from here?
- What/who is a drain on my energy?
- When in my life did I feel the most comfortable, energized or excited? What was I doing?
- What is my authentic self?
- What are the wishes I have, or had, for my life?
- What feeds my soul?
- What is preventing me from making positive choices for myself?

During my inventory I discovered some small things. I decided to let my hair grow. I always wanted to, though I was told it did not look good or wasn't proper for someone my age. This process gave me permission to wear it the way I wanted, and I am happy with how it looks and feels.

I connected with things I used to love doing as a child—paint by number, daydreaming. I confirmed the joy in some of the things I was already doing—working jigsaw puzzles (which helped me get through the first few months), knitting, walking, felting. I have expanded some of these, taking more walks with friends, taking classes to learn new techniques for my felting and new ways of making art.

I also learned that I was finished with some of my volunteer work, and I had the luxury of quitting a job I had thought about leaving for a couple of years. I have always been selective about friends—choosing those who contribute to my well being, as I do to theirs. I dropped people from my life when I realized the relationship didn't feed me and that I was giving more than I was receiving. I now focus on friendships that are reciprocal, have an easy give and take, and do not require extra work on my part.

What I have learned was not revolutionary, though it helped me refocus my energy on what is important. Doing an inventory can help us throw out what we do not need or want: draining relationships, stale environments, the negative thoughts of other people. Sometimes we have to shed parts of ourselves, just like a tree sheds its leaves to allow for new growth. The loss has taken something away: a spouse, a child, a sibling, a friend, a lifestyle, a job, a house. We love and miss what was, and we still go on living. What do we want life to look like? Life after loss is time to dream. We should not judge our answers.

Taking an inventory does not mean we are now obligated to do everything we think of. It helps us to make the most of our life, not necessarily the most of our time, which implies being busy and productive every minute of every day. It helps us reconnect with what is important and let go of what does not energize us.

We also have to recognize that doing something for ourselves is not selfish. It is self nurturing. At times we may have an inner voice that says "I can't__ because___." We should listen to our thoughts and ideas and choose those that will help us go forward.

This is a time of transformation.

Newness can be exciting—a new job to learn, a book to read, a subject to explore, new friendships to nurture. It is a time to fill our soul. We are beginning a new chapter with a new way of looking at, and being in, the world.

TAKE AN INVENTORY USING THE QUESTIONS IN THE PRECEDING TEXT
AS A GUIDE.

It is not easy to find happiness in our selves,
and not possible to find it elsewhere.

∞ Agnes Repplier

Chapter 7

Taking Care of
Our Body

It is very easy to not take care of our body when we have experienced a loss. It is easy to fall into hours and hours of sleeping and self-medicating with alcohol or other substances. It takes energy to get up, shower, dress, exercise, and eat well. In some ways, though, taking care of our body can be the easiest aspect of going forward. It is one area of our life that we can control and make choices about what to do. Get out of bed and take a shower. Take a moment to feel the water run down our body. Allow our self to be comforted in the water. It is okay to cry and talk in the shower. It may be the first place we start feeling. I made a promise to myself that I would start the day as I had always done—to experience something of the routine I had in my "old life".

We can step out of our home and walk one hundred yards or as far as we want. As we go along we can feel the earth, listen to the birds, hear the traffic, see the colors around us. Focus our attention on everything.

One of the things I cherished was when my friend asked me to walk with her. I got out and I moved. She encouraged me to talk as we walked. I was lucky enough to have three people in my life who asked me to walk. If no one asks, ask them, set a date and keep it. If you do not like walking, choose something else that you enjoy doing that will get you moving. Ask someone to join you.

About three months after Ben's death I decided I needed to have some structured exercise. I had never belonged to a gym and did not like the atmosphere there. As it turned out, a couple of months before his death, my daughter and I ran into a friend of hers who owned a Pilates studio. I found that information and connected with a wonderful teacher for weekly, private lessons. She was very understanding and gentle with me. A few months later I convinced my husband to go as well, and this new commitment to myself has brought me health, strength, and a sense of calm.

After the loss is the time for some "comfort food." Our wonderful neighbors went around our cul de sac and asked people to drop off food for us. By doing so, two things happened: we were fed wonderful homemade food from all over the world, and our neighbors learned of our loss without our having to tell them. When we had eaten the food and returned the dishes, I found some normalcy in cooking food. We can buy our favorite fresh foods. Prepare them simply. Sit down at a table and focus on tasting each bite while knowing we are taking care of our self.

Sleep can be difficult. We may be afraid to dream. We might not have made peace with our self and keep reliving the past, or we may want to escape through sleep. I didn't have trouble falling asleep, though I found it hard to stay asleep. If I woke from a dream, it helped me to write it down, so I would not keep reviewing it as I tried to return to sleep.

I also created a scenario in my mind of walking down a beautiful beach. I would envision what I was wearing and what the sand felt like. I knew in the scenario that I was meeting my husband at the end of the walk. When I was having trouble going back to sleep I would think of this same scenario, and over time I was able to sleep before walking the entire length of the beach.

I know in the beginning I did these things with tears in my eyes, overwhelming sadness in my heart, and aches in my body. As I continued these activities my body responded and lessened my physical pain.

WHAT DO YOU NEED TO PAY ATTENTION TO ABOUT EATING OR SLEEPING?

WHAT HAVE YOU NEGLECTED IN YOUR PHYSICAL SELF?

_____

_____

_____

_____

_____

_____

_____

_____

_____

_____

_____

_____

_____

_____

_____

WHAT STEPS CAN YOU TAKE TO CHANGE THAT?

_____

_____

_____

_____

_____

_____

_____

_____

_____

_____

_____

_____

_____

_____

_____

Chapter 8

Solace

Solace is finding comfort in a place or activity. Nature has always been that place for me. As a teenager, I thought of becoming a park ranger. I fantasized about spending every day in a beautiful setting. Nature shows me the ebb and flow of life. Birth, death, and rebirth. The leaves change and drop and then come back to life in the spring. They never stop. They keep pushing on. The ocean waves continue to roll ashore whether they are big or small, if it is windy or calm. They go on.

I am fortunate to live near the Pacific Ocean. The drama of the coastline, the redwood trees, and the variety of animals that call this area home all help me connect to the vastness and feeling of awe that life brings. I feel rejuvenated when I spend time amidst this ever-changing landscape. As I write this I am sitting in a cozy room, listening to thunder and rain, watching a swollen river rush downstream. Lightning just flashed. And now hail. I feel calm, contentment and yes, joy. In experiencing this beauty and power of nature I find comfort.

When Ben died I was a docent at Ano Nuevo State Reserve, a beautiful piece of coastline where northern elephant seals go to play, molt, and breed. Otters drift in the water, sea lions bark from its island and whales swim by on their annual migrations.

During the breeding season thousands of seals come ashore to fight, mate, and give birth. As docents we lead tours through the seals to educate the public on their habits and environment. Ben died in the midst of this breeding season.

I could not finish my responsibilities of leading the tours for the remainder of the season. When I returned in April, seeing the two-month-old weaned pups playing on the beach reminded me of the cycle of life. Not all of these young seals make it to adulthood. Many may return next year, though maybe not the next. Who knows how long each of us will be on this earth to continue our journey or what that journey has in store for us to experience?

Elephant seals are not very maternal. The females nurse their pups for four weeks, wean them, and then leave. Those pups are left alone to rely on their instincts. This became a metaphor for me—that on some level we are left alone to our instincts as well. We can learn things, listen, and watch others, but ultimately we have only ourselves. This helped me understand my role in Ben's death a little better. We shared parts of our life together, but ultimately, regardless of what losses we suffer, we are on our own to make our own life and decisions.

The natural world is much greater than we are, and we are all living here together and separately. Being in nature teaches me about life and puts it into perspective. It brings me peace.

WHERE, OR FROM WHAT, DO YOU RECHARGE AND/OR FIND COMFORT?

HOW CAN YOU EXPERIENCE IT MORE OFTEN?

_____

_____

_____

_____

_____

_____

_____

_____

_____

_____

_____

_____

_____

_____

_____

Conversation enriches the understanding,
but solitude is the school of genius.

∽ Edward Gibbon

Chapter 9

Solitude

Many of us are uncomfortable being alone. We fill our time with activity—shopping, eating, watching TV—anything to fill the gap.

I have always been comfortable by myself and with silence. It has a calming effect on me. It is a source of creativity and dreaming. Right after Ben's death, solitude and quiet helped me work through my thoughts and emotions. It allowed me to feel my grief and to live with the pain. It also helped me see the bits of sunshine through the fog of that grief.

Silence can be thought of as a gift, where there are no demands, whether in your head or from the world around.

Some people get to this state through meditation, though

it does not have to be a formal practice. I find, after I clear my head, I can listen to my thoughts, ideas, and feelings. Solutions to problems or concerns will become apparent. This book came from those moments of silence.

We often tell ourselves, "I don't have an hour to be by myself." Ten minutes is all we need. We can carve out that time by arriving at our destination ten minutes early. Upon arrival, set a timer on your phone, close your eyes, and sit in the silence. Have a paper and pen in your car or bag if you want to capture any thoughts. If your "to do" list gets in the way, write it down. This will help you clear your mind.

Create these moments each day. Start with when you are transitioning from one activity to another. Going forward we can make the time longer and schedule it in our day, just as we do with appointments and other commitments. We can give ourselves the moments of silence to listen to what we have to say.

WHAT DO YOU THINK OF BEING ALONE?

WHAT ARE YOU AFRAID OF DISCOVERING?

WHEN CAN YOU CREATE TIME FOR SOLITUDE?

People are lonely because they build walls instead of bridges.

∽ Joseph Fort Newton

Chapter 10

Asking for Support from Friends and Family

Most of us are hesitant to ask our family and friends for support in the best of times. Especially at times of loss, however, they may want to support us but are not sure how or what they should do. They may feel relieved when we tell them exactly what we need.

Although people would say "let me know if I can do something," "Call me if you need anything," I rarely did. It is sometimes easier to say "There is nothing you can do." I know now, though that I should have asked them to walk with me or just stop by and sit with me. We must give ourselves permission to say, "Thank you, would you please do—." Friends and family might be more willing to help right after the loss; but I am sure they would still help months or years later. As time goes on it just might get harder for us to ask.

I remember that sometimes when I cried my husband would look at me with sadness on his face, and I am sure in his heart as well. All I wanted him to do was hug me and not say anything. But he would just look at me. So one time I finally said, "Please just hug me." It was a small, easy thing to ask. I was reluctant to say it because I had not wanted to add to his grief, though I had started resenting him for not knowing what I wanted. Of course, even though we have been together for over thirty years he could not, and should not, have been expected to read my mind. Asking for that small gesture brought us closer together, and he was more than willing to give me a hug. It may have helped him as well.

The way we ask for support is important. It should allow us to get the help we need without burdening the other who may be experiencing their own grief. Many times when we feel the need for support, we are feeling emotional—sad, angry, confused, or lost. If we do not express our true feelings they may continue to build or have negative results. Be open and honest.

Tell others what you truly need. They will be helping us and themselves.

WHAT KIND OF SUPPORT DO YOU NEED?

_____

_____

_____

_____

_____

_____

_____

_____

_____

_____

_____

_____

_____

_____

_____

_____

_____

Who can you ask?

_____

_____

_____

_____

_____

_____

_____

_____

_____

_____

_____

_____

_____

_____

_____

WHAT WOULD YOU SAY TO THEM?

_____

_____

_____

_____

_____

_____

_____

_____

_____

_____

_____

_____

_____

_____

_____

_____

_____

Part III
Our Relationships

We don't see the world the way it is,
we see the world the way we are.

∞ Gandhi

Chapter 11

Being There for Others

Unless we live in a vacuum we have others close to us who are also feeling the loss. We have shared and are sharing a common experience.

In loss, our relationships will be tested.

I don't know how they came to be, but I believe the guidelines that popped into my head shortly after Ben's death have helped us to go forward.

- *No blame, no shame.* We loved Ben, and each of us tried to help him in our own way. We don't blame each other for his actions. He was on his own journey and we, individually and together, provided all the love we could. We did what we could to love and help Ben.

- *It is okay to say "I can't."* "I can't make a decision." "I can't say anything at the memorial." "I can't talk right now." And we will not ask why. There will be no judging. Even though I might want you to participate, it is fully your choice.

- *We will grieve individually and together.* We will grieve differently. We will pay attention to our expectations of each other in our grief. We will not expect our needs to be met by another. That is our job and ours alone. It is okay to behave any way we deem fit, whether it is to be together or apart, to cry, to complain, or to be angry. We will be there for each other and continue to show each other love and support.

There were times that we strayed from these agreements, though we tried to live by them and respect each other as we went through the days ahead.

It may be easy to blame others or accuse them of not doing enough to prevent or mitigate our loss. We don't know how they feel around us and how we feel around them. Can we trust them with our true emotions and thoughts? Will their pain overwhelm them, or will we provide them comfort in knowing that they are not alone? Will we be able to handle this for our self as well as be there for them?

Along with taking care of ourselves, we often want, and need, to take care of and nurture others. We have to pay attention to our family because these ties are important to us going forward. And when we help to sustain them it sustains us. We have a chance to make these bonds tighter.

My husband and I are partners. We lean on each other. We are in this together. He does not feel any less pain, any less anguish, nor any less sorrow than I do. He is not missing Ben any less. We need each other. When he cries I hold him and I am strong for that moment. When I cry he does the same for me. We have no need to say anything. He is surrounded by his grief.

It is hard to look outside oneself when we feel so much pain and when our lives are turned upside-down. But we must because we need each other. Together we can forge our new life going forward while living and sharing our new reality. Together we are stronger.

Depending on the age of our children, what we do or say may be different. I have adult children, and I ask myself, "How much do I let them see me cry?" It is important to give them permission to be sad and angry, even blaming for a time. We need to recognize the impact our behaviors and words have on them.

One of the guidelines that I offered right after Ben's death, and we continue to follow, is that we all grieve differently. We cannot judge how others handle it or show their grief. We must open our heart to them, no matter what. Everyone likes to be listened to. I try to avoid going into "Mom" mode and not give mini-lectures, but will listen as much as I can.

After great loss is a time to be gentle in our communications.

Responding gently can be a challenge. Emotions are running high, and we may be on the brink of responses filled with anger or sorrow. We want someone to hear us, listen to our grief, be present for us, and support us through our tears and worries. For those close to us, we can help provide that support as well.

Listening is an art. When I am with my family I try to be 100% present, not being personally distracted or thinking about something else or figuring out what to say. Looking at another person and nodding is not listening. We could be a million miles away in our head. This is especially true after a loss. We have a lot to worry about. When we are listening we may be in an emotional state, or what the person is saying may bring up strong feelings. They may be angry or despairing over their, or our, actions.

It can be very difficult to step outside ourselves so we are able to support and communicate with others. If we speak or act when our emotions are intense, our words may have a negative impact. Words spoken that cause harm are very difficult to take back or be forgotten. During a time of loss we are all hypersensitive, and harm can be easily caused without intention. Setting aside our emotional reactions is key; otherwise we cannot truly listen.

Of course it is all right to feel what we feel; but it's not all right to act out those feelings if they cause harm. If we cannot set them aside in the moment, we should ask to continue our interaction later and remove ourselves in order to release the emotions.

Something that helps me to defuse my emotions is going for a walk and crying if I need to, or talking to myself out loud, or even screaming after first making sure that no one else is around or will be affected by my behavior. Once I identify the cause of the feeling, I can figure out if I can control the cause. If I can, then I can figure out an action to take. If I have no control over the situation, then I must release the emotion by more wailing and letting go until it is spent.

Once we have tamed our emotions and let them go, we can start to listen. When someone else is talking I try to assume positive intent. If something is said in anger I tell myself that the speaker is in pain and is expressing it through their feelings. It is not directed at me.

I am a vehicle for receiving their emotions.

I am not meant to keep another's emotions, but rather to listen for the cause of the pain with compassion and understanding and make sure I do not jump in with an emotional response or solution of my own. This is very difficult. When I feel my emotions getting in the way I tell myself, "This is not about me. They are intending to communicate their pain and not hurt me. They are entitled to their feelings and how they see the situation."

Other people's perspective is real to them. We may not agree, though we can accept that this is their reality. Our reality is shaped by the filters that are created by who we are, what we have experienced, how we grew up, what we think of the world, how we feel at the moment, and what we believe is right and wrong. These filters become our reality, though they are really only how we see and feel our experience, our perception.

In addition to understanding that what the other person is saying is their perspective, we must also recognize when we are stuck in our own perspective. Letting go of our perspective helps us to see their perspective.

After a devastating loss it is especially important to let others speak their mind or cry or scream without interrupting or finishing their sentences. The moment is not about us. It is about them. It is hard not to give advice, or problem-solve. Our loved one is in pain; emotions are flooding in and, many times, taking over logic.

Being there for another is about listening first and then responding. What do you say? Most times we are asked to be present—to convey that we have truly heard them by being empathetic and reflecting back to them their feelings and words. Hug them, express concern, show them you love them regardless of the emotions they are displaying. Much of the communication in the early days is about feelings, not problems to solve or actions to defend. Listening, acknowledging, being present, and showing affection are often all that is needed and all that can help.

Living life is about communicating with others. How we do it can enrich our life and that of those around us.

WHAT GUIDELINES WOULD YOU LIKE TO CREATE FOR YOUR RELATIONSHIPS?

_____

_____

_____

_____

_____

_____

_____

_____

_____

_____

_____

_____

_____

_____

_____

WHAT CAN YOU DO TO IMPROVE YOUR LISTENING?

WHAT ARE SOME OF THE ISSUES THAT HAVE COME UP IN YOUR
COMMUNICATIONS?

_____

_____

_____

_____

_____

_____

_____

_____

_____

_____

_____

_____

_____

_____

_____

The thought manifests as the word;
the word manifests as the deed;
the deed develops into habit;
and habit hardens into character.
So watch the thought and its ways with care,
and let it spring from love born out of concern for all beings.

∽ Gautama Buddha

Chapter 12

Unconditional Love

One of the ideals I have always tried to live by with my family is the practice of unconditional love. I have not always been successful, but it is my compass, a tenet I strive to live by that has helped me through the years after Ben's death to continue the bond with my family.

If I become upset with something they do, I try to remember that I am not them. I can only coach them to think of other ways of looking at situations and outcomes. Ultimately they make their own decisions. I understand I cannot control the actions of others, and at the same time, when I see behaviors I do not like, to speak up in the hope of guiding them.

I continue to love and support them, regardless of the choices they may make. I can hug and reassure them when they feel down, hurt, or sad, and also when we have moments of shared joy. And yet it is still difficult to not be judgmental or see everything from my point of view.

Developing good judgment is a critical skill. It is a mental ability to practice discernment. Good judgment is the capacity to make reasonable decisions, especially in regard to the practical affairs of life. Judging, however, is a mental habit in which we form an opinion about something to criticize or censure. Sometimes we have to make a judgment and a decision. We can decide to try to guide someone to consider alternatives, but do it in a way that does not pass judgment.

To me, unconditional love is paying close attention to the people I love, to their moods and to their concerns. I work to not impose my expectations on them as to whom or what they should be. I have not created who they are. My behavior can affect them and reinforce certain aspects of their behavior, though at the core, I am not going to change who they are. Unconditional love recognizes and encourages them to grow in whichever direction they may follow.

Our love for our family is eternal and constant. We would give our life for them. We would do anything to keep them safe, to keep them close. My rules for them were not to do harm to themselves or to others. Ben never intentionally harmed others, though in the end his one act of self-harm created the greatest hurt of all for all of us.

The ultimate act of unconditional love is to forgive him.

WHAT DOES UNCONDITIONAL LOVE MEAN TO YOU?

How do you practice it?

We should take from the past its fires and not its ashes.

✐ Jean Juares

Chapter 13

Traditions and Rituals

One of our family rituals is to go out to dinner together or gather for a meal before one of us is leaving town for a vacation or to work. The last time I saw Ben was the evening before I was leaving for Japan. I cooked a crab and steak dinner for those of us who were in town.

After his memorial my older daughter had to return to her show in Sacramento, so we all decided to go out for hamburgers. It was difficult to go without Ben. He would always make a point of attending these dinners, even if it meant putting off meeting his friends. My younger daughter had a hard time stepping into the restaurant, though with my arms around her we walked inside. We ate, talked, and went through the motions. It was good to have that first public meal behind us. These rituals are important to us and help us go forward as a family.

When dealing with rituals or traditions, we have to make sure that we do not assume that everyone wants to continue on in the same way. It is important to ask if each person wants to participate, and if they want to continue in the same fashion or if they want to make any changes to what we had considered "normal"

When Ben died we had a family vacation planned in May, two and a half months later. All of us were going to Croatia and Hungary. We had been planning the vacation for over six months. His passport was on his dresser, ready to go. Family vacations have always been about joy and fun together, exploring new places. No friends or other family, just the six of us. We always looked forward to them and, because my children were in their late twenties, it had been harder and harder to schedule time. Should we still go? How would that be?

We decided to go and spend the time with each other. It was not perfect. The harmony we usually experienced on vacation was hit and miss. We missed Ben. The dynamics had changed.

The trip was a break from routine, which was good, and we had meltdowns, panic attacks, bad dreams, and arguments at different times—many emotions that we had never experienced together on vacation in the past. It was very obvious that our family was being redefined in so many ways: six to five, from four children, who had paired up in many areas as two and two, to now two and one. The concern we at times had had for Ben was no longer there and other challenges gained new life. He and our younger daughter were very, very close, and she especially missed him. We laughed, cried, and argued. But we made it.

Six weeks later, on the spur of the moment, we had a long family weekend. That reestablished our flow of being together again. That first year we were lucky to be able to share additional long weekends together. Each time it got easier, and we were able to solidify our bond and love for each other.

As with any loss we experience the firsts—anniversary, birthday, holiday—in our new reality. For us Christmas was a very special time. If we were not all able to make it on the 25th, we changed the date and had the holiday together as late as January 15th. Our tradition, ever since the children had entered their teens, was to gather in the morning, open stockings, and then play games my husband and I created with the prizes/gifts being money. Sometimes the games were physical or mental in teams or alone and of course always adding up to the same amount of winnings for each person. After the games we would relax while I cooked dinner, which we would eat in the late afternoon.

After Ben died I asked our children if they wanted to continue to play games. I knew it would be harder for my husband and me to make them. It was always something we stressed about and then had fun designing. They said they really enjoyed them and wanted to continue. I asked if we could go out to dinner instead of me cooking, as I felt that was too much for me to commit to. So a new tradition has been born: Playing games and dining out. Over the years the tradition has grown to include the children's partners. Now we make up games to involve them.

Traditions and rituals are important. They provide continuity through the year and over time. At a time of loss it may be tempting to cut off, or step back from, our traditions, or to go forward with no questions asked and dread the experience.

Communication and changes are good. Sometimes we need to remember the reason for our rituals—to be together.

WHAT IS A TRADITION OR RITUAL THAT IS IMPORTANT TO YOU?

WHAT DO YOU WANT IT TO LOOK AND FEEL LIKE NOW?

Part IV
Spirituality

In one sense there is no death. The life of a soul on earth lasts beyond his departure. You will always feel that life touching yours, that voice speaking to you, that spirit looking out other eyes, talking to you in the familiar things he touched, worked with, loved as familiar friends. He lives on in your life and in the lives of all others that knew him.

✑ Angelo Patri

Chapter 14

My Beliefs

All of us have a concept of the soul and how spirit is manifested in our life. Some of us belong to a church and follow traditional religious teachings. Others find our own place to worship and design our own ways of honoring spirit. Others have no belief in God, a soul, or afterlife. There is no one "right" way, since all of these ideas are based on belief. The important thing is that our belief system helps sustain us through life, especially when we are faced with loss.

The power we give our beliefs is part of our personal journey. My beliefs in the soul and spirit have helped me to step outside, and through, my emotions—to go forward.

I know for some there is a belief that suicide is a sin, and that one's soul will be punished in the afterlife for this, or that the person's body cannot be buried in sacred ground. We may even feel shame that our loved one took this route and feel we are now looked upon negatively by others, and maybe God. This is very difficult to overcome. People should seek guidance elsewhere if this is holding them back from going forward.

I believe each of us is on our own journey, though we are all connected as souls and as members of a soul family. I believe that our birth and end-dates are predetermined, regardless of the way our death happens. I also believe that our spirit comes to Earth to learn lessons and, as a part of a soul family, we make agreements between our souls to help us learn these lessons. Khalil Gibran said, "We choose our joys and sorrows long before we experience them." Part of being human is living through many types of losses, whether it is a job, house, lifestyle, or death.

I think the saying "Everything happens for a reason" can be misinterpreted. This sometimes takes on the meaning that we have done something to cause what happens to us, that whatever action we have taken has caused the outcome. This may be true if the loss was something we can control, but if not, this thinking leads to guilt. I like to think that the reason things happen, over which we have no control, is because we came on this earth to learn how we respond to loss, or poverty, or wealth, or whatever the "things that happen" to us may be. The important part is not what caused what happened, but how we live our life given these events.

Ben is a part of my soul family, and I believe that his spirit lives on and is always with me. I will see him again, as we are eternally connected. I cannot hold him or have a conversation with him, though I talk to him in my mind and out loud. I know he hears me. I ask for help and guidance, and I write to him. He is still here. We just have to communicate differently. I believe Ben is in another dimension where he can see and hear us. I cannot hear and see him. I visualize it like a one-way glass in a soundproof room. We are on different sides of the glass. Though we know someone is on the other side, we can't know their reaction to what we say and do. He communicates with me in his own way, not mine.

WHAT IS YOUR SPIRITUAL BELIEF AND/OR PRACTICE?

WHAT SOLACE DOES IT PROVIDE?

How do these beliefs guide you in going forward?

Miracles surround us at every turn if we but sharpen
our perception to them.
∽ Willa Cather

Chapter 15

Dreams and Signs

We all dream. Sometimes we remember a dream, or feelings from it lingers, and sometimes nothing comes to mind when we wake. There is a lot of published information about dreams and their messages. For me dreams are a way I connect with Ben. I always have a pad of paper and a pen by my bedside because I want to capture the dream as soon as I can. Many times it happens in the middle of the night.

I don't try to interpret my dreams, though I pay attention to the setting and who shows up in them. My family shows up often, and of course Ben comes through. Many times he comes to me as a child around eight years old. He will crawl into my lap and snuggle. What is interesting is that he would do that at age two and three. By eight he was off and running and our affection was demonstrated through a hug. These dreams give me comfort, and I feel he is telling me he always loved me and still does.

Right after his death I got into the habit of writing down my dreams. Here are fragments of one dream I had three weeks after his death: It is a beautiful, warm sunny day by a calm blue lake. I walk up and Ben is there. He says, "You know it was not planned–spur of the moment." I say "I know," and we hug. He and his brother are sitting at a square table. His brother says, "We had some good times." Ben says "I know", and they continue to talk. His younger sister and Ben are standing and hugging. She is talking to him while they are hugging, and Ben is nodding his head. I come up to him while he is sitting and say "You know what I am going to miss the most? Hugging you." He stands and we hug. I have a sense we have gone back in time and I don't want to fall asleep as I will lose him.

My husband had a dream before we went on our first family vacation after his death: All of us were going through airport security, and Ben could not come through. He was fine with it and he gave the impression he had to wait to go through and could not go with us. To us that meant he knew we were going away and that he was with us, though not in a physical way.

In addition to helping us come to peace about loss, dreams can also help us solve problems that may have been caused by our loss. We can conjure up the issue in our minds right before we fall asleep and then write whatever thoughts or images appear to us as we wake up. Sometimes even a quick thought may unlock an answer to our problem. This can be helped by our intuition.

Everyone has and uses intuition.

We get a gut feeling about a situation. A tiny voice tells us we should do something or avoid a place or be cautious of a situation. I am listening more to my intuition. I have always been lucky and can clear my mind very easily. Now, most days I move though the day without actively thinking and go wherever I am drawn, whether it is to a task or an activity. Of course there are some things I must accomplish in the day. In the "in between" moments I let my intuition guide me.

Besides dreams and listening to my intuition I find myself paying attention to small things that happen. I believe these are things that Ben is orchestrating to show he is around us. I know this can sound far-fetched and not rooted in logic, but it is part of my belief systems. I call these occurrences signs.

Here are a number of examples:
- When my mother was making phone calls for me after Ben's death, she put her phone down. When she refreshed it Ben's contact page showed up.
- Right after his death I would wake up with the song "(Sittin' On) the Dock of the Bay" going round and round in my head. I men-

tioned that to one of his friends, and he told me Ben loved that song and he would sing and dance to it.

- Awhile later, my husband and I would smell cigarette smoke. Neither of us smoke and no one was smoking around us, though we could smell it, especially around our desk area. Ben smoked. We continue to get this scent from time to time, mostly around our desk, though we also smell it three hundred miles away at his grandparents' house.

- I picked up a work assignment a year and half after Ben's death. I was traveling a great deal, and in the evening I would eat by myself. I noticed that when I thought of Ben a little bug would fly around me. I could be in a high-end restaurant or in my hotel room and it would appear. I then started noticing the little bug would show up when our family went out to eat together. I never thought the bug was Ben, but I would have a feeling that Ben had sent it to keep me company.

Every day I wake up and wonder if Ben will connect with me in some way. I now pay more attention to the people I meet, the things I see, and where my attention goes. I walk with a heightened awareness.

HOW CAN YOU INCREASE YOUR USE OF YOUR INTUITION?

WHAT DREAMS DO YOU REMEMBER?

How can you increase your use of your intuition?

WHAT DREAMS DO YOU REMEMBER?

WHAT SIGNS MAY HAVE APPEARED THAT YOU HAVE NOT PAID ATTENTION TO?

First we have to believe, then we believe.

∽ G.C. Lichtenberg

Chapter 16

Blessings

Many things in my family's life have changed since Ben's death. I had often read that good will come from a loved one's death. I think that is a terrible way to think of what has come our way. Good things have not happened because he died, though I have come to believe that he has helped orchestrate blessings for us.

The first blessing was for my younger daughter, who was very close to Ben. She had an on-again off-again relationship with the man she wanted to be with for the rest of her life. At the time of Ben's death, they had broken up for good. When her love heard the news about Ben he was on a business trip. He flew to her side. He made a commitment then and there that he would not leave. Four years later they married.

My life is very different than it was before. I am now running a nonprofit, writing this book, and have a vacation home. I doubt any of this would have happened without Ben's death and the way it changed my reality. I have learned that we don't search for our life's purpose; it finds us.

After Ben's death I quit my job as a corporate trainer. I had become bored with it, though never made the decision to quit. I was very fortunate to be in a position that we did not need the income. About a year after Ben's death I told my husband I wanted to do some kind of work, partly to challenge myself to learn something new, and partly to see if I could still get up in front of people and speak. A third reason was to get out in the world traveling by myself again.

Two weeks later I got a call from a woman I knew, though had never met, offering me a four-month job training reps for a coffee company. I only had to commit to one year with an option for two more years. Perfect, I thought. Training vendors about coffee is very different from training executive teams in interpersonal skills, so I did it. I enjoyed the travel, had the little bug to comfort me, and felt that I had regained my presence and voice in front of a group. I was still very good at what I did. I signed on for the second four-month assignment, racked up 75,000 miles, and decided that was all the work I needed. I had asked, and the opportunity came. After working short stints for two years, I discovered I was really finished with the corporate world and retired for good.

Two years after Ben's death, my husband and I went on a cruise to Australia. Part of the experience was to meet with psychic mediums. I have always believed that some people have a gift and can communicate with those that have passed. One such person was Deborah. We met her at dinner as she sat next to my husband the first night. Getting to know her better throughout the week, we felt she would understand Ben, so we asked her if we could schedule a private reading with her.

When we started our reading with Deborah, the first thing she said was, "Who has—?" stating a very specific attribute of Ben's house-mate at the time. Ben said to thank him for being such a good friend. Deborah went on to relay many specific things about what was going on with Ben's friends and our family.

Ben told us his friend was writing a song, which was something we had found out a couple of months before the trip. He talked about our tradition at Easter of cracking eggs on each other's heads. He said that I would write this book and he would help us find a vacation house. He mentioned people by name who are on the other side with him. He talked about what our vacation house would be like. I really felt that I was talking to him and could ask him questions.

Deborah is not just an amazing medium, she has also become a cherished friend. I feel Ben helped put us in each others' path. I feel very comfortable in being able to contact Deborah if I ever feel the need to connect with Ben and have done so about once a year.

I know Ben and I are still linked together and that he is aware of what is happening in our lives and is with us every step of the way.

My vacation home was not something I was actively seeking. I had mentioned to my husband my desire for a place where we could all go as a family and spend time together, but we had not even discussed it. I knew I wanted a place in California, near water, and within a drivable distance. I had not come up with a budget. Occasionally I would search the internet and would religiously review the real estate section of the Sunday paper.

One Sunday, a couple months after our reading with Deborah, I saw an ad in the paper for a property on the south Fork of the Eel River in Mendocino County, at a price I thought was affordable. The ad included a picture of a farmhouse with a lawn around it. I had never heard of the town that was listed. The bottom of the ad had a phone number and said "Call Ben." I stared at the ad as chills ran through my body. Call Ben. I had to pay attention.

I showed my husband the ad and told him I wanted to investigate the property. I did some searching and found the town and the property for sale. This led me to the website of a real estate agent. It looked like the same house in the pictures, and the description matched, but there was no mention of anyone named Ben.

I did nothing for a few days, though all the while thinking of the property. The website had said that there were also two smaller houses that were rented on the property and it seemed we could make it work financially. I told my husband I was going to call the phone number. When I tried to reach Ben the phone rang a fast busy, as if it was a wrong number. So I emailed the realtor, who verified that it was the same property and that the owner's name was Ben. He gave me a different number to call.

It just happened that our wedding anniversary was coming up in a week, and I convinced my husband that we should take a long weekend to see Ben and the property. We found a wonderful heritage hotel called Benbow Inn to stay at to celebrate. It all seemed rather surreal.

Finally our Sunday morning appointment came and we met Ben. The first thing out of his mouth was "How did you find me?" The paper had printed the wrong number, and no one else had called about the property. We took a tour of the property, and for me, it was like a dream come true. Eight acres, three houses (two in great shape, one that needed renovation), a building for a game room and my felting studio, a river, and redwoods. Ever since coming to California at age seventeen I have always loved and felt at home amongst these giant trees.

We got home and immediately decided that we should make an offer. Two and a half months later it was ours. Financially it worked out perfectly. We have a lovely couple with two small children as tenants who watch over the property and help care for it. My studio is a wonderful setting for making my art. We are having fun rebuilding the small cottage as a guest house. My next-door neighbor is a fellow fiber artist, and we have wonderful dinners with her husband, a gourmet cook. I feel so welcomed and at home there.

I am not sure I would have paid attention to the ad or quit my job as a corporate trainer if I had not been living in my new reality. I miss my son every day. I continue to cry at times. That hole in my heart opens and closes. I am thankful for the blessings we have received since his death. I believe he has sent them our way.

WHAT BLESSING HAS COME YOUR WAY AFTER YOUR LOSS?

HOW DO YOU EXPRESS YOUR GRATITUDE?

_____

_____

_____

_____

_____

_____

_____

_____

_____

_____

_____

_____

_____

_____

_____

_____

You Don't Have To Do This Alone

Sometimes we need and/or want to talk to someone outside our family and friends. There are many wonderful people out there ready to help.

If you want to talk to someone one-on-one consider searching the web for therapists/psychologists in your area. Most therapists will let you visit with them over the phone or in person for an interview. Find the one that you can relate to and that feels right for you. There are many clearing houses that provide lists and profiles. Here are a few of them:

www.psychologytoday.com
www.goodtheraphy.org
www.findapsychologist.org
www.helppro.com

If you would like to join a group, search for counseling groups or grief groups in your area. Many churches, hospitals or community centers sponsor such groups. Here are a few:

www.kara-grief.org
www.griefshare.org
www.hospicefoundation.org
www.compasionatefriends.org

If you found this book helpful, please consider a donation to The Ben Fund.

www.thebenfund.org.

You will be helping to pay for counseling for young adults twenty to thirty years of age who live in my community.

Your donation it one hundred percent tax deductible.
Thank you.
Lisa WolfKlain

About the Author

Lisa WolfKlain is the mother of four children and has been married to her husband since 1979. They live in Foster City California. She has a BA in Social Welfare from University California Berkeley.

As an international consultant she worked with executive teams to improve performance and inter-personal skills. She also was a Vice president of Human Resources and Wellness for an insurance company running an alternative medicine health plan.

Lisa served as board chair of Community Overcoming Relationship Abuse and was on the boards of Family Support in the Workplace, The Northern Peninsula Chapter of the ACLU and The Institute of Naturopathic Medicine. In 1993 she was inducted into San Mateo County Women's Hall of Fame.

She currently spends her time with her family and is an avid fiber artist. She also runs The Ben Fund, a non-profit she and her husband set up as a legacy to their son, Ben, who passed away in 2011.

CPSIA information can be obtained
at www.ICGtesting.com
Printed in the USA
FSHW02n0501221018
53060FS